Copyright © 2016 Fabian D. Falls. All rights reserved.

No part of this book may be reproduced, stored in a retrieval system, or transmitted by any means without the written permission of the publisher.

All Scripture quotations, unless otherwise noted, are taken from the King James Version Bible.

First Published by Fabian D. Falls

www.createspace.com/6019134

Fabian Falls

PO Box 27843

St. Louis MO 63146

ISBN 978-1523655144

Talking Hands

FABIAN D. FALLS

Copyright © 2016 Fabian D. Falls

All rights reserved.

ISBN: 1523655143
ISBN-13: 978-1523655144

ACKNOWLEDGMENTS

I thank God for the great gift of writing. I thank my Lord and Savior Jesus Christ for saving me. I thank God for my wife and all of my family and friends for supporting me. I also would like to thank in advance all the many souls I will be able to reach by the gift and anointing that God has given me!

PEACE OF MIND

Powerful thoughts cross my mind

As I think about peace all the time

I think about nations living with war no more

I begin with love as the eagles begins to soar

I see such a beautiful thing

As I set out to explore my dreams

I seek to be a trendsetter and set the captives free

And not worry about the consequences that may happen to me

One precious soul- one at a time

Giving to them the same way I got mine

I seek to spread happiness by living in peace

Being gentle to someone with the words that I speak

Open the door for you when you walk in

Shake your hand as if you and I were friends

Not allowing my past to dictate who I am

But living in love capturing what I am supposed to see

Powerful thoughts cross my mind

A thought of living in peace and love all the time

LOVE MADE TIME STAND STILL

Love is exactly what it is

It is a moment captured in time that holds the way you feel

Love is sharing and caring and holding hands

It is like holding someone's heart in the palm of your hand

It is sweet gestures and watching movies real late

It is the most romantic notion that your mind can create

It is laughing when you laugh and shedding tears when you cry

It is meeting something that's impossible and for you I will try

Love is standing next to beauty and you know its distinct smell

You can be blind, but when love is around you can definitely tell

When love is around you don't keep up with time

You are busy playing and gazing into each other's eyes

Love is exactly what it is

It is a moment captured in time that holds the way you feel

Love seems almost motionless, but yet love is so real

Life is so beautiful because love made time stand still

I LOVE POETRY

I have never seen so much joy

I have never felt so much peace

I have never heard so many beautiful things

Until God let me look inside of me

I have never seen a world inside of dreams

I never had visions to things unseen

I never rode on a cloud

Until the gift from the heavens came out of me

I have never seen peace move through the air

I have never seen words make some start to stare

I have never felt emotion

Until I saw poetry everywhere

I never really lived until I began to live

Until I expressed in words what I really feel

I never knew my heart until my heart knew me

In love with the love that poetry poured out to me

THE BEST IS YET TO COME

The best is yet to come

And I am truly having fun

I have seen both sides of all the different emotions

I have seen the stillness of peace and drama of plenty commotion

How do I see all that I see

When I close my eyes I can see things that are far from me

I can see me capturing life as it tries to escape

I can see time stand still when I am almost late

I can see beautiful things in the midst of ugly dreams

I can see disaster turn quite remarkably into wonderful things

I can see the plans for my fall, setup and doom

But somehow it vanishes away and love seem to fill the room

The best is yet to come I can hear this voice say

I have shaped you and molded you for this day

The best is yet to come so I am yet holding on

Claiming even through my weakness I am very strong

THE SNOW DANCE

The mountains of life and the glory of the story I tell

I saw the snow dancing in the air as it so quietly fell

I studied its demeanor and it seemed to have an attitude

Nothing harsh and nothing too rude

As the snow fell and gathered with one another

I looked in amazement at all this beautiful weather

As time passed by more and more I saw

One snowflake with the other snowflake- they seemed to be at war

Even through all my speculations I heard the snowflakes say

I am the persuasion that brings you out to play today

When all of the war was over I saw not one casualty

It was a beautiful arrangement of nature captured inside of me

PEN CRAZY

I think I use the word crazy a lot

I use it whether things are good or not

I think about a situation and say that it is crazy

But will the sane and educated know what I mean

Most of the time I mean what I say

But how am I using this word today

I write and write and then I write some more

I guess that is crazy to some and then I still write some more

I love to express what is inside of me

It is an artist depiction of words in life I see

It is the canvass that holds no limitations inside

It is like my very own heart having a set of eyes

It is crazy the way I am able to write all the time

It is like a pen or a typewriter with its own mind

It is like a gigantic dictionary and computer inside of me

Painting life's true picture so beautifully

READ BETWEEN THE LINES

Out of the things that I see

Why is this so different to me

A botch out of a batch no one else can see

Transparent but yet so noticeable to me

I see the unique color scheme

Jacuzzi tub as if it was a dream

As the lights brightly shined through the night

I envisioned me in the park flying a kite

A mystic voyage that I brought from the past

An excursion of an assignment I had to have

Taking a shower with no curtains, but I see the glass

I see the scheme of the colors I noticed in the past

How deep is it that brings me back to reality

I see the botch in the batch no one else can see

TRUTH IS THE VERDICT

Sometimes things are not the way they seem

You can think things are one way from the things you've seen

But have you truly seen what you were supposed to see

And are you living the way it was meant to be

Things are sometimes different from what they appear

Don't always act on what you hear

For what you hear might not be truth at all

And what you claimed to see may not be what you saw

Never judge someone on what you feel

Your true emotions may not be real

It may be as unreal as the truth that resides within you

Or as reliable as the most outrageous lie ever told to you

Some things are not what they appear to be

Are you truly focused on what you claim to see

If you look within can you truly see

And accept the reality of what's to be

Can you live a life full of deceit and lies

If the truth in you continues to hide

F.Y.I

I had never heard such an unbelievable thing

Water intoxication it was something I didn't believe

Could you actually drink too much water at one time

The answer just blew my mind

I thought that you could consume as much water you wanted to

I found out different, so I wanted to educate you

There are so many different things to learn in life

And to relay truth is something extremely nice

I would rather spread notions about positive things

Rather than gossiping and spreading lies and negative things

So once in a while you read something I write

And it is not the normal flow of the things you like

Just remember that I get excited when others educate me

So just as informative I want to be

THE ART IS FROM THE HEART

Do people ever get tired of me writing poems

Because as I complete one I am ready to write another one

Do people think I talk too much

Always talking about writing and poetry stuff

Do people think I write about writing too much

Or am I just making too big of a fuss

I ponder all sorts of notions at times

Just jotting down what comes to my mind

I write whatever is on my heart

I don't contemplate too much- I just paint the art

I don't use any props or safety tools

My heart is usually the only equipment that I use

I get a clear pathway from my heart to my mind

And it flows through my pen all the time

Do people ever get tired of me writing poems

You will just have to forgive me because I am having fun

IF THINGS WERE EASY

If the world was in love with itself and I could tell time
I would tell everyone what was on my mind
If I could explore the things within me and see more of what I want to see
I would eventually be what I claim to be
If the mountains was the opposite of very small hills
And love was the antidote that could be taken like a pill
If life was the things that lived inside of me
Then you could see my words so beautifully
If I was to write like I do all day and night
I believe I could make this world alright
If I was to continue to love all day
And I found more positive words to say
I would tell life it was time to love and to put away its arrogance
If it doesn't learn to respect others, neither will it respect it's self

IT IS REACHABLE

To be loved unconditionally

To live the best life inside of me

To shoot for unattainable goals

To know things I don't currently know

To speak unspeakable words

To say things never heard

To explore and have more than dreams

To hold in my hand unreachable things

To pray every incurable disease away

To feed the hungry every day

To be able to give the homeless a home

To tell the weak they are strong

To touch the life of someone without any hope

To see a crack addict no longer smoke

To see an alcoholic not drink any more

To see the downcast life begin to soar

To live in life a beautiful scene

To take death and doom and no longer allow it to be seen

To see in life some remarkable things

To love every one unconditionally

LOVESHIP

It is so great to know love

Love and I are best friends

We go everywhere together and we like to go on trips

And when I talk to someone love likes to speak

Love likes to do everything with me

I like how polite love likes to be

Love is the greatest friend to me

Love sees everything that I see

When I take a bashing from someone, love takes it too

For me there is not anything that love wouldn't do

When there is a problem love comes to help me out

And when someone screams at me love won't let me shout

Love has my best interest at hand

And love helps me to be a better man

Love is the greatest thing that has happened to me

And forever true to love I want to be

HERE, THERE, AND EVERYWHERE

It is amazing how you can sit somewhere

You haven't left you location, but you've been everywhere

I can travel to Paris and leave my thoughts all over Spain

Even throughout Europe people know my name

It is amazing what you can do with a pad and pen

Throughout the world I can meet new friends

It is exciting to know that wherever words can go

The perception of my thoughts others may know

It is terrific and so amazing to me

The many places my thoughts are destined to be

From South America to Africa, and all the many lands

One day billions of people will hold my book in their hands

It is not my dream to write to just the U.S.A

I want to touch every nation with magnificent love every day

CYCLES OF NOTHINGNESS

This is the mountain that I see

The task that makes everyone else begin to see

The motivation to motivate the dubious task to procreate

Life's lessons beyond the cycles past

Looking for a turtle as time seem to go fast

Life's lessons and cycles of nothingness

Why do so many fail the test

Over and over we go around again

The message we hope to finally send

Life's motivation- the true dramatic scene

The hope of one dedication of hope to dream

Why are we asking the same questions again

Not a thought in sight for a familiar friend

Will things change and will life grow away

Will I see dedication bloom to see another day

Will I touch the mountain at its very peak

Will I see the things I so desperately seek

Over and over we go around again

A powerful message we hope to send

Life's lessons- cycles of nothingness

Some things we should not do again

PAIN, PAIN GO AWAY

It seems that people don't know I am hurting on the inside

I am feeling pain because of what I see with my eyes

I felt pain when I heard of the death of my favorite megastar

I feel pain when I see a generation of children

Not thinking and not knowing who or where they are

I feel pain when negativity tries to influence the crowd

It is not just me and it doesn't have to be a mega-celebrity

Anyone's death takes a toll on me

I love to see people walking and living in love

But hatred and jealousy seem to takes its toll

Why can't we start loving again

Why do so many allow destruction to become their friend

I pray that this madness will end

And through my writing an imperative message I send

Live life learning and producing every day

And hopefully through the advancement of others

My pain will gradually go away

ALL THINGS SEEN

I am powerful and I am loving too

I am the epitome of what is destined to be

Hourglass notions as time sit still

Love inside the trophy of life's cool grill

Mount Everest or some tall edifice

The sultriness of days revealing skimpy clad dress

So much for the eyes to see

A tainted doctrine of an immoral society

So much for the eyes to see

The bewildered confession of an inanimate sobriety

I am powerful and I am loving too

I am the epitome of what is destined to be

I will not listen to the corruption of negativity's cruel lies

I have to hold on to hope and reject what I see with my eyes

I have to look past the hurt and pain

I have to revise the purpose for defeat's shameless game

I have to rise above life's greatest storm

And rely on the breeze of hope in the winter of destruction

To teach me love and to keep me warm

HOPE

Life seems to come with many different trials

It is constantly challenging us to be better all the while

Life seems to make us want to lose our hope

But I want the world to read this poem I wrote

Hope is something we should never give up

It is our anchor to believe in the dreams we trust

It is a never-ending blinking directional sign

That leads us to victory during difficult times

Hope is the jam on the sandwich of life we spread

It is the fighter of defeat that makes us lift our heads

Hope allows us to stand up and roll up our sleeves

When doubt and fear tries to keep us from the things we need

Whatever life challenge we may presently face

Don't hold your head down in despair or disgrace

Even the best of us has endured the worst of days

Don't allow negativity around you consume your mind

Hope will elevate you above the problems every time

CRIES OF DESPERATION

Moment by moment, seconds and minutes at hand

I see a cry of desperation in this land

I see slavery and bondage creeping in a very deceptive way

I see its destruction every day

Moment by moment, seconds and minutes at hand

Drug and alcohol addictions, sex, lust and violence is destroying our fellow man

How can we not say or do anything about what we see

I feel it because it hurts inside of me

How can we hate or how do we discriminate

How can we steal, kill, or destroy when we did not create

How can we be bold enough to go against our God

Lord help us to take away the pride

Moment by moment, seconds and minutes at hand

We are vessels to be used to help this land

And give our brothers and sisters a helping hand

TRUE GAIN

Clear cut solutions and eye catching strain

I struggle to look at the face of shame

Noting the destruction I look at the chance we take

To look at this deception face to face

I can give you money and I can give you prestige

This is a lie that smacks us in the face

Lies and destruction to acquire temporary gain

Is an equation that will bring disgrace to you and your name

It takes time and persistence to see true gain

Why are so many lured by this faux way of life

Because so many lack patience and direction in their life

FYI- destruction and deception is only a temporary job

And its hidden agenda is to steal, kill and rob

So don't be enticed by quick temporary gain

You have no pension plan in this horrible game

All it guarantees is more hurt and pain

Lies and destruction to acquire temporary gain

Is an equation that will bring disgrace to you and your name

It takes time and persistence to see true gain

It takes time and persistence to see true gain

COMPLEXITY OF RATIONALIZATION

Life is more than rules and regulations

It is the combination of situations that we are constantly facing

Steps of stones not yet navigated

The decision of this way or that way in life's navigation

Simple as it seems but yet so complicated

The precision of a thought- let us see the waves

Let us stay mindful of our equity in this life every day

The good outweighs this seemingly begrudging attitude

Knowing that solitude of deliverance is coming real soon

The focus of universal love and harmony

The touch of delusional thoughts playing in symphony

Its okay to dream- it's perfectly fine to scream out loud

Silence of an inner emotion in a disruptive crowd

Life is more that rules and regulations

It is the compilation of the situations that we are constantly facing

The simplicity of a perplexity in a consciousness we don't understand

A complexity of rationalization that evades no man

AT LAST

I am on a campaign to get people to read

To find out information they so desperately need

I am on a quest to influence people to stop going so fast

To slow down and enjoy the things that truly last

I am on a mission to stop all this negativity in the world

And pray for peace for every man, woman, boy and girl

I am hoping to see people loving and producing again

And see physical enemies becoming friends

I want to see love prevail and not all this junk I see

Am I dreaming or is this a reality

I want to see fear and doubt so far from me

I want to see beautiful mountains and smiles on people faces

Not sadness, sorrow, and disgust in people faces

I want what I believe God want us all to have

Hopefully one day I will see it *"At Last"*

WHAT'S INSIDE OF YOU

The love I found is not a mystery

It is the product of thing dwelling inside of me

It is emotions and happiness- it is peace and joy

It is the equation of life that brings us joy

The love inside of me makes starvation go away

It stops killings, rapes and brutality

The love inside of me makes negativity go away

And make people want to love, work and enjoy their families

The love I have inside of me drive drugs and alcohol away

It gives people the incentive to live positive and be productive every day

The love inside of me brings more than peace

It brings hope that the entire world should see

The love inside of me speaks volumes in words

About something that so many haven't heard

My thoughts are centered on Jesus Christ

And the miraculous change that has happened in my life

The love I've found is not a mystery

It is the product of things dwelling inside of me

I WANT A KNIGHT NOT DARKNESS

Many women say they are waiting on their knight in shining armor
Not men that will come lie, cheat and try to harm her
Many women are looking for men to be men
Not for lazy arrogant game players just to move in
Many women want a man to show true light
Not just for someone to come for a snack and leave at night
Many women are looking for a dedicated, committed, goal oriented man
Where is the solution to the darkness many men bring
They started out as if they were the best of friends
Many women are looking for the one to come sweep them off their feet
But in the end they are left alone by some no good cheat
I listen to the sentiments of many women I meet
And many are concerned about the things they see
They are seeking love and peace to comfort their hurt
These are the words from many women that speak
I want a knight not darkness to sweep me off my feet

INSIDE THE EMOTIONS

Gentle thoughts and tremendous adversity

In a world that seem to not even care

Will my thoughts ever go anywhere

People are walking as if they are lost within themselves

I have private battles and struggle my self

Self-help books and many conferences and seminars

Is there a radar of hope that tells you where you really are

Help I hear the cries from the inside

Scared, but yet glad to be living

How can I escape and where does my deliverance come from

Inside the emotions the thought are choked up

Inside the emotions I can really feel the pain

Life's fresh breath hoping to see change

Inside the emotions the heart continue to beat

Searching for answers that will bring meaning to the mind and streets

Inside the emotions are realizations of these gentle thoughts

Understanding that change is not free it will come with a cost

COVER ME WITH SUCCESS

Success is made for those who believe success is real

It can come into your life and alter the way you feel

It can make the weariest man become strong

It can make you feel comfort when you are all alone

Something about success that stands out in a man

It stands up and out and begins to change life's plans

Success can be viewed in many different ways

You might describe it one way and another I might say

But to be honest with you, is true success truly successful at all

Will you be ready when your name it begins to call

What is it that makes a man have true success

Is it having a lot of money, wearing nice suits strapped to your chest

My definition of success you really might not like

But I have pondered this notion day and night

Success to me is gaining reality

That there is a God greater than you and me

Success is made for those who believe success is real

It can come into your life and alter the way you feel

GARMENTS OF PRAISE

As the winter brings all the cold weather

People bring out there cashmere coats and some wear their leather

As the trees look so naked to me

Totally exposed without any leaves

I see people scraping snow and ice off their cars

People drinking hot stuff to keep them warm

It is amazing because the grass cease to grow

And where did all the bumble bees go- I guess I will never know

When it rain in the winter, it is so, so cold

And all the thousands of birds, where did they go

I don't see the millions of ants anymore

Someone said they collected food all summer and have it in store

So I guess I can learn from things that's different from me

And they don't have pay mortgage for a place to sleep

As life brings the storms and all the cold weather

I'll bring out my cashmere of faith and spiritual leather

I will put on the whole armor of God to keep me warm

And stay clothed in faith by staying in His arms

So when the coldness of life starts to confront me

In the warmth of God's loving Word is where I'll be

SEEDS OF SALVATION

I am the only one standing in the rain

I do this sometimes to ease some of the pain

As it pours down with abundance of rain

I seed my grass without an ounce of shame

Everyone else is inside nice, dry and warm

And even though I am wet I'm protected from harm

I can feel life growing inside of me

The thoughts of the blades of grass I will one day see

If I spread these seeds as it continues to rain

And if I think about love will I feel no pain

If I think about the love of Jesus Christ

Will I feel some sense of happiness in my life

As I ponder the notions of all these seeds

I think about how His love- so many people desperately need

I think about how people are dying every day

And yet so many people have so little to say

As it rain I will continue to plant seeds

Seeds of hope and compassion and prayers for people's needs

I will see a true beautiful harvest one day

From the things I've planted and the words I've said

I will see the beauty of this beautiful green grass

And also the harvest of love that will always last

I AM ABLE

I am not working doing hard manual labor

I am healthy and yes I am able

But I have been called to do a more important thing

That is to fulfill my life-long dream

I have always had the passion to create and write

To reveal the poetry of my soul portrayed through my life

I love to create powerful messages with little letters and words

And tie them together in a way that has not been heard

I love to utilize every character in the alphabet

Writing to me is like getting rest

It is exploring the greatest journey that I could ever see

It is showing the world the portrait of beauty that resides in me

In writing there is calmness that soothes the volatile

It is enjoying a special gift from God all the while

Writing to me is life's unique poetry

A gift and talent very much treasured by me

I am not working doing hard manual labor

I am healthy and yes I am able

But I have been called to do a more important thing

That is to fulfill my life-long dream

LOVE ADDICT

Watching love go to sleep as it grows

It is something that only time will know

Watching baby rabbits playing in the grass

Watching determination to succeed direct life's path

How can love be asleep and awake at the same time

I guess when we sleep love is still on our mind

I watch the movement of beautiful trees

I see beauty smiling as far as I can see

I don't focus too much on the negative things

I am addicted to love and the joy it brings

I see smiles on people's faces

I see little kids learning to tie their shoe laces

I see a kid learning to ride a bike for the very first time

I see so much beauty on my heart and mind

So as I watch life on this super-wide screen

I will continue to search for all the peaceful scenes

As I watch the spinning of this thing called life

I pray to see things more pleasant and nice

SO MUCH TO DO, SO LITTLE TIME

So many different things in life to do

So many choices and obstacles in front of you

So many times we can hardly find our way

We lose track of time and even the words we say

So many people and so many different attitudes

Some are polite and others can be intentionally rude

As life begins to shape and forms itself

Remember to always give the best within yourself

Never accept no when it comes to achieving your goals

There are no limits to the heights you can go

Mountains were meant to be moved if you only believe

You can fulfill the beautiful dreams your heart can conceive

If only you learn to always believe in yourself

You will shoot for the best and accept no less

When the complexity of life tries to confuse your mind

Remain positive and think of appealing things all the time

Live a life full of love, peace and happiness

And the strength of your joy will do the rest

TALKING HANDS

My hands are not idle they have something to say

They are motivated to see another day

As life's situations are filled with all its commotion

I will fulfill dreams with my hands and be always hoping

Hoping that my hands continue to move

Displaying words that comforts and soothes

I will be a blessing to someone with my God-given hands

Have hope to one day help my fellow man

With my hands I seek to change the world

By revealing words of encouragement to young boys and girls

I want the world to see there is victory

And God will do for you what He has done for me

I'm not trying to be boastful and I don't mean to brag

The gift that I have many wish they had

So I will utilize this gift to the best of my ability

And cherish the love God has placed in me

People say I'm not working and not utilizing my hands

But I beg to differ- I have talking hands

DO WHAT YOU CAN

Why do so many people strive to be like someone else

When they should just be themselves and always do their best

I know many people have accomplished so many different things

But you should pursue your own aspirations and dreams

If it is something to be accomplished, you can achieve the goal

There is a drive within you that only you can know

Potential for greatness is bottled within you

With all of that information, now what are you going to do

Will you sit back and watch grow without you

Or will you progress with life that's evolving around you

Will you be a help to encourage peace, love and advancement in this land

Or will you miss the opportunity and leave it to your fellow man

THERAPY

Writing is so therapeutic to me

It shows me things I wouldn't otherwise see

It is a sip of peace without the glass

It is like enjoying something I've never had

Writing to me is so much fun

It is just as exciting as watching the brilliance of the sun

Writing is a gift and a very special art

It is the hourglass of uniqueness that comes from the heart

Writing is beauty and listening to different sounds

It is as important as the world spinning round and round

It is something that I can't easily describe

It's an expression of hope that keeps peace alive

Writing is spontaneous and invigorating to me

It is the most spectacular vision I will ever see

Writing is the vehicle that drives people's heart

It is the dexterity of perfection of a thriving art

I'M A PENTER

Every time I pick up a pen

I somehow begin to meet new friends

I am addicted to bring smiles and joyous words

I am delighted and honored to be able to serve

Writing poems is not just a duty to me

It is special and respectful at times

I get excited when I am able to express in words

Something that has not been expressed or heard

I like to paint unique portraits through poetry

An expression that can be felt as people are able to see

I like to do with words what I see carpenters do

I'll pick up a pen and build a safe place for you

I hope people understand how important it is to me

A gift from God spreading love through poetry

I WOULD BECAUSE HE GAVE

If I could I would expose the atrocities

I would fight for peace with every breath in me

If I could I would change this world

I would turn mere rubbish into exquisite pearls

If I could I would improve men's quality of life

Education would improve life and make things nice

If I could I would decrease homicides and teen pregnancy

I would give people views of where their life should be

If only I had the opportunity

I would spread love the way it should be

If I had just a little bit of clout

I would give this earth something to shout about

I would let all men know about Jesus Christ

And how He gave love and added substance to my life

I BELIEVE I CAN WRITE

I want to be the Michael Jordan of poetry

When they need a go-to man they will look for me

I want to excel above every limitation set

I want book sales to go "swoosh" as it hit the net

I want people to enjoy every shot I make

And when it's time to take a shot I am never late

I want to be the Michael Jordan of poetry

When people want to see a champion read they look to me

I want to obtain many awards and even receive a championship ring

I want to soar and glide through the air

And see my books being read everywhere

I want to be the Michael Jordan of poetry

Humbly using the gifts and talents that God gave to me

RELIGION OR RELATIONSHIP

Wondrous moments once again

Powerful moments as I begin

As the nation goes through a self-perplexing war

In a land where no one really know who they are

Where everyone knows so little, yet so much

Where everyone is fighting over un-important stuff

People sometimes want to get somewhere

And yet impassioned to the clothes they wear

Is a religious war about religion at all

Or a power-struggle on who make the calls

What is a religion to a non-religious religionist

A package of wonders with doubt inside of it

What is the point to someone with no point at all

I really don't care if you want to make the calls

Promises are made as money is spent

All I want is a world with love inside of it

So if I make one dollar or a billion or two

I will pray for your relationship, not your religion and yet still love you

WHAT HAS HAPPENED TO US

After the many struggles to able to vote

After many winters without a coat

After many years of not being able to sit on the front of the bus

After many years of pure put downs

After many years of struggle, sweat and tears

After many lives lost and many beat-downs

After many years of poverty and hunger to us

After all of this what has happened to us

After watching the climb and rise of our beautiful race

I ask this question-what has happened to us

After all that was sacrificed to pave our way

To help us reach plateaus to see brighter days

After all the hardships and challenges our ancestors have mad

What in the world are we doing today

After all those beautiful soldiers who have lost their lives

For me to be able to see through these eyes of mine

After all their struggle and after all their pain

I have to ask- What has happened to us

HURDLES OVERCAME

Walking through life taking steps to succeed

You do all that you know to get what you need

Life begins to throw blow after blow

But continue to trust in the things you know

The waves may dash to and fro

And water may be splashing into your boat

Keep on dipping while throwing doubt away

Don't be afraid when your boat begins to sway

You may look at your situation and can't see the change

But deliverance comes when you call Jesus' name

It may look like help is nowhere to be found

But you will make it back to solid ground

The shore may appear to be a mile away

But keep on believing help is on the way

If you keep on trusting and don't give up hope

You will have peace and joy as you step on dry land

And get to hold on tight to your Savior's hand

And when you are rescued your life won't be the same

You will be able to share with others about hurdles overcame

EXCUSE ME YOUR HEART IS SHOWING

Out of the abundance of the heart the mouth will speak

With eyes of your heart it will seek

Your heart can tell me many different things

If you are happy, nice or just down-right mean

You can tell a tree by the fruit it bears

You can see it plainly anywhere

You can see if an apple came from any other tree

You wouldn't be you and I wouldn't be me

Our heart can truly allow us to expose ourselves

It can take those hidden agendas and put them on the shelf

The heart is such a revealing thing

It can take those hidden thoughts and make them seen

It can bring out the best or even the worst in you

Show you up by the things you do

Out of the abundance of the heart the mouth will speak

With the eyes of your heart it will seek

All that is visible your heart is exposing

Excuse me your heart is showing

SOMETHING IN ME

It is a blessing to express what I feel inside

The thought of me still being alive

I know that I could have died years ago

But there was something in me God wanted the world to know

There is a warrior- a great fighter inside of me

A drive within to the best I can be

I am to move in directions I've never seen

To do the impossible accomplishing my hopes and dreams

I am to live a life I dreamed about when I was a kid

And live a reality that my dreams said I lived

I am to tell the young people to educate themselves

Don't listen to doubt or anyone else

You can do it because God said you can

I would rather listen to the Creator than listen to man

It makes no difference what obstacles comes your way

Be a mountain-climber everyday

Fixate in your heart the mind to create

And through persistence and diligence you will be great

It is a blessing to express what I feel inside

Just the thought of me still being alive

I know that I could have died years ago

But there was something in me God wanted the world to know

I SEE CHANGE

I hear the sounds of distant lands

I hear the strength of a humble man

I see the love and warmth of a mother's love

I see the Spirit descending in the shape of a dove

I hear a child cry and see another child play

I feel the love of peace every day

I hear peace telling violence to stop

I see compassion ticking on every clock

I see the joy of a rainbow even through cloudy rain

I see hope calling out your name

I see peace for all the world's troops

I hear laughter of joy of a loved one coming home

I see the lonely never being alone

I feel the love that God has created for all

I feel happy for those who answer His call

Love without ceasing is what I want to the world

Love every, man, woman, boy and girl

POETRY! HERE I AM

I have been sent to touch the world with poetry

An art from Heaven that has been granted to me

A gift more precious than any classroom can teach

More dynamic that a great orator can speak

Poetry is more than a pad and pen

It is a connection between enemies and friends

Poetry is peace that comforts the soul

It is a love so unique the God himself had to show

It is not demented expression, but its sweet music to the ear

It is the eloquent sound that you precious heart can hear

It is a love worth risking everything to save the authority it has

I thank God He allowed poetry to cross my path

While so many appear to want to abuse this great art

I will continue to let its beauty pour from my heart

Even the first amendment won't persuade me to taint this unique treasure I have

It is the covenant of greatness, love and honor that will change life's path

It is the greatest vision that can be seen with the eye

God sent Israel, Moses- Poetry! Here am I

DO NOT ENTER

If trouble is what it appears to be

I want to keep it very far from me

I don't want additional problems to interfere with my life

I have enough headaches and deal with too much strife

If trouble tries in, I have to keep trouble out

I don't want to know or hear what it's talking about

I have to continue to seek to have a peaceful life

And stay close to those things that are calm and nice

I don't need too much excitement or explosive things

Just to peacefully and quietly pursue my dreams

I try to live and treat people with love and respect

To be kind and gentle as I pass life's tests

I want to be a man of true integrity

And have those that know me be confident of me

I want to say what I mean and mean what I say

Love to love peacefully every sing day

I want the issues of life to be smooth throughout my day

And let trouble move and get out of my way

IF THIS WORLD WERE MINE

One sound and profound gesture I see

And how glorious will our lifestyle be

If life could somehow take on wings

And in this life we could do anything

When it doesn't matter rich or poor

Anyone everywhere had their pantries full

Healthcare for the young and the old

That's right the uninsured could even go

When education was paid for as long as you wanted to go

And taxation was the fair way for all to grow

When people flourished in business and had the upper hand

But they did not deny helping their fellow man

Where everyone understood how important it is to learn

And that increase is not always what you earn

When affordable housing was equally made

And just as needed we were rewardingly paid

One sound and profound gesture I see

And how glorious will our lifestyle be

If life could somehow take on wings

And in this life we could do anything

NO MATTER HOW, NO MATTER WHEN
NO MATTER HOW, NO MATTER WHEN

Sometime I seek to know life's end

I wonder the how and sometimes the when

I wonder sometimes will I touch someone by the life I live

And when I am dead and gone, how will people that knew me feel

Will those that I hurt find forgiveness in their heart

Will my words affect anyone by me exercising this beautiful art

Would all the suffering and sacrifices be all in vain

Will people know who I was or better yet, Jesus' name

Would I have put on the hearts and mind the things I wanted to

How much of it will not be in vain

I wonder if I have persuaded someone in life to make positive change

It would be a very beautiful thing for me

If I have helped someone spiritually or emotionally

If I have left a notion of warmth and love

Then my life would have been the success I thought it was

If I have touched a soul to begin to love again

Then it makes no difference the how and when

SPEAK INTO MY EXISTENCE

As I sit here once again pondering positive notions

While the world seem to be consumed with all its negative commotion

I view life as an opportunity to learn

To finally understand the weight of our words

To see what type of impact they have on life

To be loving with our words and very precise

It is amazing the power the little tongue has

To speak life or death into our paths

To speak a blessing or either a curse

Something beautiful or something worse

I view this opportunity as a moment to earn

 The trust of love's presence I so desperately yearn

As I sit here I am totally amazed

How people are dying every day

How war seem to be something that is glorified

How some are prospering from deceit and lies

As I sit here once again pondering positive notions

While the world seem to be consumed with all its negative commotion

I view life as an opportunity to learn

To finally understand the weight of your words

PRICELESS GAIN

The best thing I've found in life is love

I found out how priceless it is how inexpensive it was

Love to me doesn't equate to material things

It is a beautiful portrait that my heart has seen

Love to me does not have price tags

It is like trapped water finding a new path

It is a section of a puzzle fitting tightly together

It is snuggling together in really cold weather

Love goes beyond the surface of tangible things

And searches the depths of hopes and dreams

It is the climax of the most emotional high

It is the precise persuasion of peace that will not lie

Love is like light because it exposes itself

It is like a SOS signal when you need help

It is a flare that alerts the yearning in your heart

It is filling everything you need in your emotional shopping cart

The best thing I've found in life is love

I found out how priceless it is and how inexpensive it was

Love to me doesn't equate to material things

It truly is the most beautiful thing that I've ever seen

PRESSING FOR THE BLESSING

There is a place we need to be

But most of us want it to come with ease

No hard work and no sweat involved

We want God to move now and our problems be solved

God is concerned about character and integrity

And much more involved with the things we can't see

We are looking for material things

While God is viewing eternal things

While we are seeking finances and things in the physical

God is sculpting love and peacemakers not the immoral and immaterial

Don't look for the quick fix or the easy way out

Let the hard times make you still praise and shout

When the good times or the bad ones comes your way

Tell the Lord I am going to praise you anyway

I'm not quitting or throwing in the towel when Satan starts messing

I'm holding onto God and pressing for the blessing

TRANSFORMERS

There are many people in the world

With many voices from everywhere that can be heard

But until we hear the voice of God

Our true disposition and destiny will continue to be robbed

Until we get to the point where we love God's Word

And we are truly transformed by what we learned and heard

Until the Word of God can be like a mirror in our face

Until it shapes and mold and transfigure everyday

God's Word is like a scalpel in the Surgeon's hand

It will sift the impurities out of your dirty land

God is not in the business of creating more performers

God is diligently loving and creating transformers

GIFTS THAT BLESS

God is great at blessing us with gifts

But so many try to use gifts to bless themselves

I know it is a great thing to be gifted by God

But I don't want to be a hypocrite and secretly rob

I don't want to rob others and rob myself

To be gifted by God and use my gifts for myself

We are gifted to be a blessing and our gifts may bring us wealth

But don't let you gifts be a curse but a blessing upon yourself

YOUR HEART SHOULD SPEAK LOUDER THAN YOUR MOUTH

It is amazing to me the things I hear and see

But I pray daily that God would build our integrity

So many people bragging about knowing the Lord

But when it comes to truly loving it seems so hard

We can't stop sinful and carnal behaviors after all these years

Still gossiping, cheating and consumed with doubt and fears

We all have some growing to do

Made mistakes and fell short I have too

But there comes a time in all of our lives

When the Holy Spirit and our love for God comes alive

We should not want to be involved in the things we used to do

There should be a burning to do right inside of you

Temptations may come but your love for God should kick in

There should be something inside of you that gets tired of sin

There should be love and commitment that goes with the dance and shout

Your heart should speak louder than your mouth

LORD I THINK YOU

A brand new day you have made

Lord I think You

A million thoughts thrown my way

But when I think you my enemies must behave

Perfect peace- when I think you

Whatsoever things are pure- when I think you

When I'm at my weakest then made strong

I think you

When the world seems to be against me

I realize who's for me- Lord I think you

When it all registers what you have done for me

Lord when I think you

My soul thanks You

YOUR WILL BE DONE

Help me Lord, I truly need your help

Sometime it seems as if I am going through all by myself

I need your touch send me an Angel from Heaven now

My mind is in agony and I am pondering how

How will I make it through these tumultuous times

I know you are there so give me strength

and courage in my heart and mind

Grace me with your Mercy as I pray like my sweat is turning to blood

You are my only hope so send me comfort from high above

I could try to battle, but Lord I can't fight alone

Nevertheless, not my will, but yours be done

MANKIND MATTERS

White on black, black on white, white on white or black on black

Brown, red or yellow- let us look at the facts

Death is such a destructive and terrible thing

Especially when it comes from someone else's hand

I don't care who are what the perpetrators are

This junk we're experiencing has gone too far

Entire city government cover-ups- crooked cops

Secret organizations or Individual cover-ups

It makes no difference it is time for change

This day to me just don't feel the same

Lord my prayer is on this day

Is that you will change the hearts of many some kind of way

Touch the hearts of the people on earth

And let them know you created them with value and worth

Destroy every work of darkness and touch the souls of man

So they can live out your perfect will loving their fellow man

GOT LOVE?

The greatest thing that could ever happen to us

A deliverance and a peace and the ability to trust

To be able to take the good times along with the bad

All the tests and setbacks this past year that we had

We have seemed to be beat and bashed in so many ways

But through it all we have survived those hurtful days

On today let us all be thankful and celebrate

Because God gave us victory for what He wanted to create

I can finally say I can live, love and forgive

I can love and pray for my enemies no matter what they did

I finally realize that love is truly greater than me

Because God is love and love dwells inside of me

WHEN GOD SAYS NO

So many people can't seem to phantom the thought
That our God can't be hoodwinked or bought
We have to understand that He has a greater purpose in mind
Instead of just giving us what we want all the time
Sometimes we really don't need what we think we need
We have to be broken from our selfishness, pride and greed
So many people actually get upset at God
Because we think we've been shortchanged or robbed
Because of His love for us we don't get everything we want
He has a better and greater purpose for all of us
So while we are complaining about the things we need
Just thank Him for strength and the ability to breathe
Don't always complain and think you should always have your way
He knows the best, sure and purest way
We have to understand that He has a greater purpose in mind
Instead of just giving us what we want all the time
Sometimes we really don't need what we think we need
We have to be broken from our selfishness, pride and greed
Don't be so quick to pack up and go
Don't lose your blessing or your witness when God says no

UNMASKING SATAN'S LIES

It is time for the truth to be told

It seems that the enemy has so many people in a hold

It appears that many are trapped and cannot escape

Many were caught in a trap while they were continuing to play

Pity pat- Pity Pat is the name of the game

So many are playing frivolously with this dangerous thing

Excuse after excuse trying to explain how weak they are

When the Lord promised He will be with you no matter near or far

If he can keep us hooked on the things of the world

He can destroy our little boys and girls

If he can keep you playing while you should be praying

He won't do anything but keep on preying

It is time out for all this that I see

It is time for us to wake up and be who God called us to be

Pity pat- Pity Pat is the name of the game

So many are playing frivolously with this dangerous thing

It is time for us to stay close to the God we serve

And develop an intimate relationship and stay in His Word

With the Word of God and prayer we can have the victory

If we stop playing senseless games with our enemy

HOW TO HANDLE TEMPTATIONS

No and then no and then no some more
It is time for us to start slamming some doors
We have done it once and time and time again
But it is time to say no and shut the door my friend
When temptations come we have the power we need
The Holy Spirit in us gives us everything we need
Now it comes to the choice that you know you must make
To be honest sometimes it comes down to being real or fake
No and then no and then no some more
It is time for us to start slamming some doors
We have done it once and time and time again
But it is time to say no and shut the door my friend
When temptations come we have the power we need
The Holy Spirit in us gives us everything we need
Now it comes to the choice that you know you must make
To be honest sometimes it comes down to being real or fake

THE VALUE OF A SOUL

One million dollars or fifty-three cents

How in the world could we put a value to it

The soul of a man is worth more than the body's crusty shell

A battle is waging for it between Heaven and Hell

The value of a soul is worth more than we think

If you don't believe me then think of this

If Jesus had to be beaten and whipped to save your soul

If he had to endure mental anguish to keep you from Sheol

If Jesus had to die such an horrendous death

You soul must be valuable for Him to endure all of this

To be mocked and abused and by His own refused

He died and suffered for you not to lose

Through His life and death and to His very last breath

He thought of you and your victory and nothing else

He died that we might live

And that we might live a life of victory and have peace for real

One million dollars or fifty-three cents

How in the world could we put a value to it

He endured more than we would ever know

His love for us showed us the value of a soul

THE DIVINE DESIGN

Uniquely fashioned and molded with the highest craftsmanship

The utmost quality of wisdom assigned to it

Your life is purposeful and you were created to shine

His divine wisdom and love were placed in your mind

Made in His image and His plan to prosper you

To be shaped into something exciting and new

His plan is for you to escape all of the enemy's tricks

Uniquely fashioned and molded with the highest craftsmanship

He saved you so that your true life will come forth

So that the entire world will see your true worth

You were created to love and show the affection and glory of God

Your life is purposeful and you were created to shine

His divine wisdom and love were placed in your mind

He desires to have an intimate relationship with you

And through that connection work out His plans through you

Through the Word of God and prayer He want His message to be heard

So that others will be transformed by His Living Word

COMMUNICATE OR DISINTEGRATE

In marriage or any other relationship

The bulk of the relationship should include communication in it

There should be times of non-physical intimacy

The laughter and joy just of each other's company

Just as people like to talk and see what's going on in life

This should be equally shared between a man and wife

So as the story is told the story is also heard

With joy you listen to every single word

It should be a pleasure to learn and discover the heart of your mate

To find out what makes them happy every single day

Sometimes you may listen and other times you may talk

Sometimes you may agree on issues and other times you won't

But however and whenever we must continue to communicate

Without it our relationship will begin to disintegrate

There should be times of non-physical intimacy

The laughter and joy just of each other's company

With God and man this balance we should create

It is up to us to communicate or disintegrate

THE BATTLE FOR YOUR MIND

There is a battle for your mind

A constant battle to capture your attention all the time

One way pulls you to the good and the other towards the bad

There is a pull on you to lead you towards immorality

That will get you hooked on negative images and distorted sexuality

Through mainline media and entertainment

The twisted view of reality has already been sent

Movies, books, music and the internet

Has played a major role in the shaping of it

The battle for your mind in this social and culture war

Is a destructive plow from Satan no matter where you are

The scheme to get you away from the things of God and his ways

To lead you into sin and have you rebellious against God everyday

The Bible is the truth and Jesus is the way

But there is a battle to lead you in another way

There is a battle for your mind

A constant battle to capture your attention all the time

The scheme to get you away from the things of God and his ways

To lead you into sin and have you rebellious against God everyday

The Bible is the truth and Jesus is the way

He will lead you into victory if you let Him have His way

For additional copies go to:

www.createspace.com/6019134

Fabian D. Falls

PO Box 27843

St. Louis MO 63146

FABIAN D. FALLS

Made in the USA
San Bernardino, CA
01 February 2017